T0078096

THE ANSWER

Tom Mangino

authorHOUSE

AuthorHouse™
1663 Liberty Drive
Bloomington, IN 47403
www.authorhouse.com
Phone: 833-262-8899

Published by AuthorHouse 04/18/2022

ISBN: 978-1-6655-5730-6 (sc)
ISBN: 978-1-6655-5735-1 (e)

Library of Congress Control Number: 2022907757

Print information available on the last page.

Any people depicted in stock imagery provided by Getty Images are models, and such images are being used for illustrative purposes only. Certain stock imagery © Getty Images.

New American Standard Bible (NASB)
New American Standard Bible®, Copyright © 1960, 1971, 1977, 1995, 2020 by The Lockman Foundation. All rights reserved.

This book is printed on acid-free paper.

CONTENTS

FOREWORD

This story has taken me over 25 years to write,
and without the love and support of my wife,
Maria, It would not have been written.

We hope John's story will bring
you closer to the Lord.

Chapter 1

THE EMERGENCY ROOM

John knew something was terribly wrong. He was in a strange place and activity was taking place all around him. The light streaming down from the ceiling above him was somehow too bright, the people in white smocks moving to and fro all around him were in too much of a hurry. The atmosphere was charged with sights and sounds and smells, which could only mean one thing. He was in the hospital, he was in the emergency room, and instinctively he knew, he was dying. Lying on his back looking up at the light, his mind began rewinding the events leading up to this moment. But weather he rewound too far or just couldn't concentrate, he found himself back as a child, and he was afraid, deathly afraid.

He was five years old remembering how his mom would call out while standing on the front porch. Johnathan Clark, you come inside this instant, time for dinner. Johnny would gently release the bullfrog he was playing with and in a wild dash to the steps, Johnny would bound onto the porch in one giant leap. His mom smiled at him and how obedient her son was. John was always being told by his mom and dad what a good boy he was. Janet and Mike Clark were wonderful parents who had instilled Christian values and polite manners in their son. Mike for his part was always playing practical jokes on his wife, often roping Johnny into these schemes. One of these times Johnny remembered, his dad whispered so his wife wouldn't hear, Johnny, drop a little ice cream on the floor during desert, make it look like an accident. OK dad, Johnny replied. After dinner was over Janet asked, who wants ice cream for desert? Both Mike and Johnny said I do in harmony, then smiled at each other. Johnny always ate ice cream with his spoon turned upside down before putting it into his mouth. Mike winked at Johnny, just then ice cream fell to the floor. Mike yelled a t Johnny in a very stern voice, what's wrong with you? Haven't I told you a million times to eat your ice cream with the spoon facing upwards? Johnny looked down and began crying, making it look oh so convincing. Mike, Janet said, he is just a little boy, why would you yell at him like that? She wrapped her arms around her son who was crying on the outside but giggling on the inside. Mike looked at his son and said, Johnny I'm sorry ice creamed at you. Johnny said that's OK dad, next time I'll have a banana and split. As they both started laughing out loud, Janet realized she had been pranked. Very funny you too, the next time you get ice cream it will be sundae. At that Mike went over to his wife and hugged and kissed her, while Johnny wrapped his arms around both his parents legs.

Johnny would look back and cherish those moments even now, while lying on his back strapped to a gurney wondering what was happening to him. The shock was beginning to wear off and he became aware of excruciating pain running thru his body. Someone stuck a needle in his arm as someone else wiped blood from his head. The white gauze had turned bright red when the nurse pulled it away. John felt pressure on his skull as bandages were being applied. Then he felt something different. There was a sharp pain deep in his chest which became unbearable. John lost consciousness and slipped back into his dream world.

Chapter 2

THE ONE THAT GOT AWAY

At fifteen Johnny was an extremely curious child. He liked being alone and would wander along the river which wound it's way lazily past his house. He had an adventurist free Spirit and he loved fishing the deep holes in the river looking for small mouth bass. During the dry season in upstate New York, Johnny would wade out into the shallow water which was easy to traverse, and mentally map out those holes. Looking at the bank for trees or bushes which coincided with the locations of those, Johnny knew exactly where to fish when the water was high. Johnny loved the outdoors and he especially loved trees like the old willow which sat right near the rivers edge. He would climb that tree and sit in it's branches for hours on end. The willow didn't seem to mind Johnny sitting on his limb, and actually Johnny felt connected to the majesty of old man willow. His mind would wander to the point where he became something totally different. Sometimes a bird or a squirrel looking down from those branches. The willow with his finger like roots jutting out from the bank right down to the waters edge, seemed always thirsty, Johnny thought. Kind of like himself, always thirsty for the knowledge of where those elusive fish were hiding. He giggled when he thought how funny the willow, so close to the water yet never knowing what was gliding past him right under his nose below the rippling surface. Then Johnny's imagination ran wild, and he became the willow, looking down at himself and thinking how funny Johnny, so close to the water trying to catch fish, and he knowing from his great height looking down and seeing just where the fish were. Johnny shook himself out of the trance he was in and laughed a great booming laugh at the irony of himself.

Johnny was an average looking boy at fifteen, some would say he was quite handsome. One of his admirers was the neighbor girl Sarah, who lived just down the street. John remembered how Sarah had asked him if he would take her fishing sometime. Being a polite boy and some what intrigued by Sarah taking notice of him, he said sure, maybe next week when it gets a little warmer. Johnny was always thoughtful of others that way, he knew spring in New York was chilly and he didn't want Sarah to catch a cold. He was looking out for Sarah's well being. This day the chill crept thru his whole body, and he gave a little shutter. He was glad Sarah wasn't with him today, but he was also a bit sad because he really did like her. Maybe it was those tiny freckles on her face that grew bigger right before his eyes as the sun shone on her. Or maybe the little dimple on her right cheek every time she smiled at him. Her light brown hair matched his own color almost perfectly, as if a painter had used the same brush on both of them while painting their portrait. At five foot six, Sarah was just about four inches shorter than he was. When Sarah looked up with her big brown eyes, Johnny felt she was gazing into his very soul. Johnny would quickly and shyly look down. Sarah was slight, bordering on the verge of skinny, But Johnny thought she was just perfect. As Johnny was thinking of Sarah, he got a nibble on his line. He instinctively jerked back on his fishing pole. The line danced from the water into the air and his pole bent like an archers bow. The next sound he heard was the sweetest of all for any fisherman. The drag on the reel clicked and wheezed zinging a tune. He had him, woo hoo, and he was a big one.

Easy boy, Johnny said to himself, don't lose him, easy does it. He gently pulled back on the pole and knew he had set the hook perfectly. Yes he had him right where he wanted him. As he began to reel in this giant he was thinking, wait till Sarah sees this monster. Just then the bass jumped out of the swift running water about fifteen yards away. Wow, Johnny screamed, he is a big one. Johnny waded a bit farther into the river to get closer to his prize when something happened. In his excitement he did something so foolish that he would soon regret it. He ran towards the big fish reeling as fast as he could, so as not to lose him. Then in an instant he lost his footing on the slimy stones of the river bed, and before he knew it, he went down. His hip boots rapidly filled with ice cold water, chilling him to the bone. The shock of his perilous situation soon set in as he fought to regain his footing, but to no avail. He was caught in the swift current and was going under water again and again. He gasped to catch his breath each time he bobbed to the surface. Just as soon as his head came up, down he went again, each time being pulled further and deeper in the icy grasp of the river. Johnny knew in his heart he may not survive this dilemma he was in. The over whelming feeling of dread fell on him as he was pulled rapidly down stream. Johnny wondered how and when this would all end. The when came with a thud as Johnny went from speeding down the river to a complete stop, knocking the breath out of him. A huge tree which Johnny knew very well from previous fishing trips was under the water, it's roots just under the surface, had grabbed him and held him fast. When the river was low, that tree would jut above the surface, but now it was completely submerged. The swift current pinned Johnny against the gnarly roots of that tree, and the worst part was he was under the water.

Cold afraid and fatigued with no hope, he did the only thing he could do, he prayed. Oh it wasn't a prayer asking God to save him from the situation he was in. No, this prayer was much, much deeper. Lord forgive me my sins, I'm sorry I let you down. Please comfort my parents as I die, and Lord and let Sarah know I really liked her and am sorry I won't be taking her fishing. Finally Lord, I commend my soul into your hands. The prayer lasted less than an instant, but in that instant weather in his mind or not, Johnny saw a hand grasp him and lift him up and out of the river onto the bank. Choking gasping and coughing trying to catch his breath, Johnny could think of only three words. Thank you God.

Chapter 3

SARAH

Just as quickly as John was on the river bank, he was back in the emergency room again, wondering how did I get here? Looking at the hospital staff working on him he noticed a sadness in their eyes. Did they know what he knew in his heart? They were fighting a losing battle. He closed his eyes again and dreamed about dating Sarah. After a few fishing outings with her, John knew he was hooked. Their like for one another soon blossomed into something bigger. Sarah would softly lay her hand on John's arm when she was making a point. Sitting on the stools at Milts Shake Shack Sarah would lean into John ever so slightly the aroma of her perfume driving John crazy. Sharing a shake at the counter, Sarah's leg would brush against his sending shivers thru out John's body. He would blush and his face would turn red. That summer went by like a whirlwind with John and Sarah spending more and more time together. While walking home from school one sunny afternoon in September, John worked up the courage to take Sarah's hand in his. She looked up at John and smiled, John knew he had landed Sarah.

It took more than a week after he had held her hand for John to ask Sarah to the senior prom. They were sitting on a park bench sharing an ice cream cone when he just blurted it out. Sarah will you be my date for the prom? Knees shaking and eyes on his shoes, he really didn't know what her answer would be. He need not of feared, as she took his hand in hers and said, there is no one else in Heaven or on earth I'd rather go with. Yes I will go with you.

The night of the prom was like a fairy tale come to life. John walked up the stairs to Sarah's house, flowers in hand. Sarah's mom and dad met him at the door smiling, they really liked John and it showed on their faces. Sarah will be right down John, won't you come in, asked Sarah's mom. Her dad shook hands with John and asked how the fish were biting. John answered saying, since your daughter has been accompanying me I've been spending most of my time baiting her hook. Her dad laughed and said to John, can't you find some how to worm your way out of that chore? They both just giggled at that, as they walked into the house. After a few minutes, an angel stood at the top of the stairs, at least John thought so. John said wow. Sarah was wearing a pearl white dress which perfectly contrasted with her dark tanned skin. Her hair was up show casing her beautiful face. It seemed to John as if she were glowing. As Sarah made her way slowly down the staircase, John could only hold his breath and watch in awe. Somehow in that moment John just knew Sarah would be his wife one day. As John handed Sarah the flowers he commented how beautiful she looked. Sarah reached for the flowers and her hand brushed his, in that instant, that slight touch, Sarah also knew she would be Johns forever. That night was magical for John and Sarah, a night either of them would not forget. They had many firsts that night. Their first dance, holding hands for hours on end, and later, on Sarah's front porch, their first kiss. After that kiss John looked into Sarah's eyes and said, that was the first of a million. They hugged each other tightly until the porch light blinked and both knew Sarah's parents were ending the date. As John waved good bye and walked down the stairs, he felt as if he were floating in mid air. He wasn't paying attention when he walked into the street right in the path of a speeding car. Those headlights were so bright and so close he almost didn't get clear. Clear, was the next word John heard, then a flash of light and a jolt went thru his entire body from head to toes. Lights flickered then shown bright again. We almost lost him. He heard some one say and then he slipped back into another memory.

Chapter 4

TRUE LOVE

After high school John and Sarah both enrolled in the community college for various reasons, mainly so they could stay close to each other. School flew by like a whirl wind, one year down, two years down, then Sarah and John each decided their futures. John was going to major in forest management, his ultimate goal was to become a game warden. Sarah's dream was to become a nurse. It wouldn't be long before her dream became reality. After fast tracking her education she graduated in three years. She applied at a local hospital and with in a week Sarah was hired. John was so proud of Sarah he took her out to the fanciest restaurant in town.

The meal was excellent, and Sarah couldn't stop blushing as John complimented her on her new job and how proud he was of her. During desert Sarah wondered why John started fidgeting so much. She asked him if every thing was alright. He answered yes, well no, I mean. John was so nervous about what was going to happen next he began to shake. Sarah, he said while getting down on one knee and reaching into his pocket to produce the most beautiful ring Sarah had ever seen. Sarah, he said again, will you be my wife? As Sarah reached out her hand and took the ring, she put it on her finger then hugged John looked into his eyes and said, yes, I'll be your wife.

As John heard the words Sarah spoke, he heard other words as well. Three words he never would have believed would be said about himself. We're loosing him! Just as fast as John's dream life was unfolding he was blinded by lights that wouldn't let him concentrate. It was like looking into the sun. Why couldn't he move his hands and arms to embrace Sarah. It was too much for John to comprehend, was his dream life with Sarah just that, a dream? His life was slipping away but that dream came rushing back.

After graduating at the top of his class, John applied to the New York State game management division. The interview a week later with George Markam, went very well. John was told to wait for a call, so he went home unsure of what that call would be. A few days later John's phone rang, after answering hello he heard George Markam say, John I'm sorry, Johns heart sank, then he heard the rest of George's sentence. Sorry I haven't called sooner as I was occupied with some poachers. John, George continued, we would be honored if you would join our team. John was so excited he dropped the phone and yelled to Sarah who had just walked thru his door. Honey, honey, I got the job. Sarah ran into his arms and said, I'm so proud of you, when did you find out? Jolted by that question he remembered George was still on the phone. He quickly picked up the phone and began apologizing to George. Don't bother George said, get back to celebrating with Sarah. I'll see you tomorrow at eight a.m. congratulations, I know you will be an asset to our team. Good bye.

Chapter 5

DEER ANGEL

The wedding plans were filled with hopes and dreams for the future. John and Sarah agreed the ceremony just had to be outdoors, and what better place than down by that lazy river. John's uncle was a priest who insisted on performing the wedding for them. Sarah's sister Sophie was so happy when Sarah asked her to be maid of honor. John's best friend Dave, was proud to be best man. You see, Dave and Sophie had liked each other for a long time. Well maybe more than liked. As far back as first grade when Dave sat behind Sophie in class and tapped her on the shoulder, she would turn around and Dave would make these funny faces. Sophie would start laughing uncontrollably and the teacher, Mr. Allen, would begin to scold her. Dave would rescue her from a long lecture by make believe sneezing over and over. Mr. Allen would forget Sophie's lecture and turn his attention to Dave. Sophie saw Dave as her knight in shinning armor from then on. Wasn't it amazing when in a few short weeks at the wedding of his best friend, Dave would ask Sophie to be his wife. And she, at her own sisters wedding would say yes. As the day of the wedding neared, Sarah seemed to be living in a dream world, much like John in that hospital emergency room. Sarah was dreaming and planning their future together, while John was dreaming about his first adventure, or should he say misadventure, as a game warden.

John could see the glare from the ice on the lake below him as he peered thru the dense fog surrounding the mountain he had climbed hours before. As he gazed downward, he perceived something dark moving across the ice which had formed on the lakes surface. Taking out his binoculars and focusing in on the dark object, a deer was plainly making it's way out on the ice towards the distant shore. About fifty yards from the shore John watched as the deer fell thru the thin ice and began flailing in the water. John quickly sprang into action, racing down the slope at a reckless pace. He knew the deer would be worn out from all the flailing trying to get back onto the ice, and would surely drown with in a short while. It took John no more than twenty minutes to reach the edge of the lake. Assessing the situation, he quickly took some rope from his back pack and attached it to a tree near the shore. Tentatively John walked onto the glimmering ice towards the deer. As he neared the hole, the ropes length ended just ten feet short of the deer. John had to make a big decision, and as he watched the deer go under the freezing water, he made it. Letting go of the rope, John crouched down on his hands and knees, and moved to the edge of the hole. He arrived just as the deer popped his head up probably for the last time. John reached down and grabbed an antler, then dragging and pulling he seemed to get an extra boost of adrenaline. The deer put one then another front hoof on the ice near John. That was all the help John needed. With a quick and powerful tug, the deer was up on the ice and rushing towards the shore. With a huge sigh of relief, John slowly rose to his feet and began walking towards the shore on the same path the deer had just taken. Then the unthinkable happened, with a sharp crack, the ice under John's feet gave way. In a flash, John thought back to that ole river he had nearly drowned in, and wondered if he had some how cheated destiny. And now in a weird twist of fate was about to repay that debt. As he fell thru the ice, he hit his head on the shelf and a sharp searing pain engulfed him. A crimson color was clouding his eyes and he knew he was bleeding badly. The pain seemed to abate rather quickly as the freezing cold penetrated his body. John tried to assess the trouble he was in. If he couldn't get out of that freezing lake with in a few minutes, he would die. John was here before and knew exactly what to do. He closed his eyes and again beseeched the Holy Spirit to intervene and save him. John's amen was heart felt and loving. He reached for the ice shelf trying to climb up and out of the frigged water. His strength gave out, he could neither get anything to grip onto or have enough strength to pull himself out. John closed his eyes and knew the inevitable was about to happen, he would perish. Just as he gave up all possibility, an amazing thing happened. Something brushed his face as he began sinking. Instinctively he reached out to feel what it was, the rope he had left behind. John had walked just far enough following that deer, that the rope he had tied to a tree was at hand. Grasping the rope, and using the last of his strength, John tugged and pulled himself out of the water and slowly crawled to the shore. John knew he wasn't out of danger yet, as he would freeze if he couldn't get warmed up. Using all the skills he had learned in training, John gathered some twigs in order to build a fire. He made a little birds nest of small twigs, then some larger sticks were near by if he did get a flame. Taking his flint kit from his back pack, he struck a few quick strikes. After about five minutes of striking that flint, some sparks fell onto the birds nest, then the kindling began to smolder. Blowing gently on the twigs they began to smoke, then a small flame erupted in the twigs. John realized he wasn't out of danger yet. He crawled along the shore gathering bigger pieces of wood which he placed on the fire. He looked on as the flickering little light began dancing into bright flames. The crackling was music to his ears, and the heat emanating from the blaze, not only warmed his body, but also his soul. John basked in the warmth of the fire, and he thanked God for again saving his family from pain. As John began to warm up, he started to feel the pain pounding in his head. He reached up to feel a gash on his skull, the pain became a fuzziness, then he fainted.

George Markam last heard from John about two hours ago, when John called him on the radio from the mountain. He had communicated to George that he was heading down to the lake to check on a deer which had fallen thru the ice. John was to check back in one hour, and when George hadn't heard from him he had become more concerned with each hour that had passed. George called Sarah at the hospital and voiced his concern to her. She immediately asked George to pick her up so she could accompany him to search for John. Sarah felt in her heart something was terribly wrong. George agreed to get her and together they traveled in the company's four wheel drive truck to John's last location on the mountain. The logging road they were on was loaded with ruts and roots, so the drive was slow and very bumpy. Sarah began to pray for help finding John. Holy Father, please guide me to John and keep him safe from all harm. George stopped the vehicle and taking a bearing on his compass led Sarah to the over look of the lake where John had first spotted the deer. John was no where in sight, as George peered thru the binoculars. The lake below had frozen over and showed no signs of life. George and Sarah didn't know where to start looking for John. That's when a strange but wonderous thing happened. As if the forest had come alive with sound and movement, a big buck ran right past George and Sarah, and started descending the mountain. Sarah yelled to George, follow me, as she took out after the deer. The going was not easy, but that deer stayed just enough ahead of them so that he was always in sight. Sarah was praying all the way down that rugged terrain. Suddenly the woods opened up, and that deer was standing near a smoking but dying fire with a lump next to it. As the deer fled, Sarah knew her prayers had been answered. John's head was badly gashed and he had lost a lot of blood. Sarah quickly went into action, taking John's temperature, which read eighty eight degrees. Barking orders to George to get the dying fire blazing, and to keep it going. When the fire was sufficiently hot, Sarah took off John's clothes, and checked him for any breaks or bruises to be addressed. Finding none, she bandaged John's head and held him close to her and the fire. After about a half hour, John responded to Sarah's gentle voice. John, can you hear me? Who am I? In a small shaky voice she would hear, you are the love of my life.

Chapter 6

THE WEDDING

It seemed like just moments ago when he heard those frightful three words, we're losing him. The next instant he heard stand back, clear, a jolt like lightning cursed thru his body to his very soul. He stiffened and fell silent. Time seemed to stand still as John slipped back into his dream. The wedding was so joyous as friends and family gathered together to celebrate. Sarah was giddy all morning, her bridesmaids were telling jokes and having fun, just glad to be with Sarah. Sophie, Sarah's sister and maid of honor, was also Sarah's best friend in the whole world. She was always making silly faces just to make Sarah smile, and this morning was no different. Sarah would remember the times when they were little girls and their mom would call them down for lunch or dinner. Sarah, their mother would shout, but Sophie would answer. Yes mom. I didn't call you Sophie, then from down the hall Sarah would reply, yes mom. Very funny you two, wash your hands before dinner. Both girls giggled away as all thru the meal they would act like the other, driving their mother crazy. Sophie was so happy when her sister and John had asked her and Dave to be maid of honor and best man. Dave was John's best friend who just happened to be Sophie's boy friend. Sophie couldn't stop smiling while she was gliding around taking care of all the wedding arrangements. Sophie was especially proud Sarah had asked her to plan all the decorations. Sophie, with Dave's help, decorated the back yard where the wedding was to be held. She had black and white balloons scattered around the yard by the hundreds. They were floating on the trellis, the trees, the fence, and even from the house. The chairs were placed in a semicircle around the arch, covered in flowers, where the ceremony was to take place. Sophie had planned for one hundred and twenty chairs, just enough to accommodate all the guests. The back yard was large enough to handle all the food tables, the cake table, and the gift table. The guests would form two lines on either side of the buffet table, which Sophie provided, so everyone could get their food with out inconvenience. The menu would be chicken breast in a marseilles sauce, tiny roasted potatoes seasoned to perfection, green beans with sliced almonds, ceasers salad, fresh baked rolls with butter, coleslaw and cranberry sauce. Sophie had even planned the shrimp and scallop appetizers, which would be served by waiters dressed in tuxes. The drinks would be flowing freely and Sophie even thought of sparkling cider for the children. The cake Sophie ordered was exquisite, with three layers of white cake and a raspberry filling between each layer. The top tier housed a perfect mini replica of Sarah and John dressed as bride and groom. Sarah loved Sophie, and when she saw all the beautiful decorations, she told her so. Sophie, you are the best sister the Lord could have blessed me with, thank you for everything you've done. Sophie told Sarah, it wasn't all my doing you know. Just then, Dave came into view carrying a last minute item, the gift box. Here is the work horse who really helped a lot, Sophie said. Dave just smiled and said hi to Sarah. Sarah ran to Dave and gave him a great big hug, almost crushing the gift box.

She whispered in Dave's ear, have you asked her yet? Dave whispered back, this is your day, tomorrow is Sophie's birthday and I'm taking her to her favorite restaurant. That's when I'll ask her. Hey, Sophie yelled, don't you know it's impolite to whisper? OK, OK Dave shouted back, I'll get back to work.

John had been out of bed since six a.m. which was his habit as a game warden. The early bird catches the worm, and that was just what John had planned for this, his wedding day morning. Instead of worms though, John was planning on catching fish. Off he went, to visit the old willow, down by the river. What more important day to visit his old friend than his wedding day. As John walked along he thanked God for all the blessings he had received since that fateful day he had almost drowned. John's mind was swirling with thoughts of this, his wedding day. Sarah was the best thing that ever happened to him. He was thinking how beautiful she is, and how she had supported him with his career. John's thoughts went back to the day on the frozen lake, when Sarah had found him, and nursed him back to health. He thought of Sophie and Dave, knowing they also would be getting married. John was a little disappointed that Dave couldn't join him on this mornings fishing trip because he was helping Sophie with the decorations. That sad thought disappeared when the fish hit his bait. John's face lit up in a great big smile. Then he remembered the day the big bass had reeled him into the river. This time, older and wiser, John slowed down and purposely walked backwards while reeling in his catch. He thought to himself, older dog, newer trick. After his third catch John looked at his watch, nine thirty. The wedding was at three, I better go clean up.

Sarah was excited about the honeymoon her and John would share. They were going to the Bahama's for a full week. Sarah's parents were graciously paying for this all inclusive jaunt. That's how much they liked John. John's parents were paying for the reception, that's how much they adored Sarah. On his way home with his catch, John stopped by a neighbors house, and gave them the fish. John was always thoughtful and generous like that. He knew this family was having a hard time and this meal would help them. Mrs. Jenson asked John if he intended to get married today, as their invitation had said? Yes he said, and assured her he would be on time. As John entered the house, his mother implored him to get showered and dressed if they were going to be on time. OK he told them, it seems everyone is more concerned than I am about making it to Sarah's on time. As John and his family pulled into Sarah's driveway, Dave and Sophie were waiting to greet them. Dave showed John that he had the ring, while Sophie gave John the biggest hug ever. She whispered in his ear, I'm so proud to have you as my brother in law. Dave chimed in, hey Sophie, don't you know it's impolite to whisper? As he chuckled. The wedding was magical, as the band was playing the song Sarah, John and Dave came out of the house. Everyone was clapping and smiling when John and dave walked to the trellis, where the priest was waiting. With a hand shake Father Thomas said to John, today you and Sarah become one, always remember that. Father slapped Dave on the back and asked, well what are you waiting for? Sophie won't wait forever you know. Dave just winked at father. Just then the music stopped and a familiar tune, here comes the bride, began playing. John went into a trance when he saw Sarah for the first time that day. In her wedding dress she looked more beautiful than ever. Trance he said to himself. The dream ended as the jolts he now felt were real. People were hurriedly moving around him, when he heard these words, He's back. John once again tried to get his bearings, then he remembered he was back in the hospital. John was afraid, mortally afraid, not just his condition, but how dire the situation was. John had been in a few life and death situations in his life, but this was something totally new. He knew deep down that this journey he was on, he would not be returning from. John's gnawing fear was the unknown. He began grappling with the thought that everything he had done in his life wasn't good enough. He was fearful that his soul wasn't clean enough or pure enough to enter into God's presence. Then as if a light switch had been turned on, he remembered God's words. Even though filthy rags, I will make you white as snow. John became aware that the devil, even now at the last, was deceiving him.

He remembered what the bible said, resist the devil, and he will flee from you. A blissful peace came over John, he fell back into his wonderful dream.

John heard himself saying I do, and Father Thomas said I now pronounce you man and wife, you may kiss the bride. John took Sarah into his arms and kissed her. The whole yard erupted with the sound of clapping, and real joy spread over the guests. The reception was marvelous, the meal scrumptious, and the band devine. Sarah and John danced with all their family and friends, who genuinely loved them. Then when the time was just right, they said goodbye to all their guests, thanked Dave and Sophie, and ran through the crowd to start their honeymoon.

Chapter 7

JAN

The flight to the Bahama's was at ten a.m. the next morning. That night at the hotel was magical as John and Sarah couldn't stop smiling. They were so happy that all other thoughts slipped away. While at the airport, John could sense an unease in Sarah. She had never flown before, and nerves were getting the best of her. John had flown once before, out west to receive special training for his job. As they boarded the plane, Jan, the head stewardess, could tell right away that Sarah was anxious. She showed them to their seats, and took a minute to chat with Sarah. Jan asked Sarah if she had ever been a passenger in a car. Sarah said yes, why? Because this is no different, just sit back and enjoy the ride. Jan put her hand on Sarah's and Sarah felt a peace come over her. She didn't know Jan was praying for Sarah's well being. As the plane taxied towards the runway, John told Sarah to hold his hand tight. As the plane started to accelerate and lift off, Sarah did just that. As the feeling of floating came over her, she heard John say, hey not that tight. He giggled at the look in Sarah's eyes as she was both excited and afraid at the same time. Soon the jet leveled out and John started getting feeling back in his hand. Sarah was now smiling from ear to ear. This is great she said to John, look we are above the clouds. John looked out the window to see white puffy clouds below, and way below them, a blue, blue ocean stretching out forever. Jan came by with the drink cart, took one look at Sarah and John holding on to each other, and exclaimed, You two just got married, didn't you? Yes, Sarah shot back, how did you know? Jan said I remember that same look when I got married two years ago. Sarah asked Jan if it was hard leaving her husband while she was flying, and isn't he afraid for you? Jan told Sarah she had met her husband on an oversea flight. He was the pilot, and while taking him lunch, the plane had lurched with some turbulence and she had spilled the whole tray on his lap. Jan said she was so embarrassed, that she just kept apologizing over and over until the pilot, Jack, said you can make this up to me. Go out to dinner in Paris with me and I will forgive you. Jan said it's a date. Only after they were married did Jack confess to me that he had lurched the plane on purpose. Sarah was laughing when Jan told her she would have spilled the lunch on him even if the plane hadn't lurched, just to meet him. At that Jan and Sarah had become instant friends. The rest of the flight was awesome as Jan kept checking in on John and Sarah. Jan showed them special treatment with snacks and drinks. When the plane started to land, Jan took the empty seat right next to Sarah and held her hand, to keep her calm and steady. As they were disembarking the plane, Sarah gave Jan a big hug and thanked her for everything. Jan smiled at Sarah and winked at John while rubbing her hand. May God bless you both.

The Bahama's were unbelievable, with so much to see and do. Riding the jet ski's were the most fun for Sarah, as every time John was behind her, she would gun her throttle and drench him. He would act all mad and Sarah would just laugh and laugh. Once when they were stopped and Sarah was reaching her hand into the crystal clear water, John had paddled his jet ski right beside her. Positioning his jet right at Sarah, he quickly hit the ignition and gunned it. Sarah looked like a drowned rat. Sarah turned to John with the maddest look she could muster, then she started laughing. Touche', monsieur pussycat, was all John said.

John's favorite activity was whale watching, and from the big tour boat, he could look right down on them. This reminded John of ole man willow, when John would sit on a limb and look right down at the fish in the river. The boat was equipped with dinning accommodations. The cost of the ride and dinner was a bit steep, but Sarah insisted they go, knowing how John loved nature so much. She was always thinking of how she could make John's life happier, and she succeeded. Being a Christian girl, Sarah was not only thoughtful and caring of others, she took it one step further. Treat others the way you want to be treated, nope, not Sarah. Treat others as God treats you was, her motto. John had fallen in love with her for that reason. John wasn't disappointed with the whale watch tour as more than a dozen sperm whales and two killer whales came near the boat. During dinner, Sarah and John talked about the days experience. John had once talked about becoming a marine biologist, but decided land animals were his passion. The meal was fantastic, lobster tails and filet mignon, with a side of giddiness from the two lovers. They were so tired when they hit the motel room, they both decided to hit the hay. John was just dozing off when he started dreaming he was back in the emergency room, but it was no dream.

A calm set in as the fear of death had subsided. With that one passage of the dirty rags, John heard Jesus whisper, Dad has not given us a spirit of fear, but of power, love, and a sound mind. With that calm came real sleep, with real dreams. He was back on the island with Sarah, getting ready for a paragliding outing. John asked Sarah if she would be okay in the air. Sarah replied, Jan will be right next to me in spirit keeping me calm. They both laughed at that statement. The rest of the trip flew by as the two just enjoyed each others company. Then the inevitable day arrived when it was time to go home. Home, that was a crazy thought. They had rented an apartment before taking the trip, but hadn't moved in yet. Oh, most of the furniture was there, and a few personnel items, like clothing and toiletries, but they hadn't officially moved in yet. When they arrived at the apartment, John lifted Sarah into his arms and carried her across the threshold. Sarah was smiling and told John not to get a hernia, after all that lobster and steak. At that they both started laughing so hard, John dropped Sarah, luckily she landed on the sofa.

Chapter 8

WELCOME HOME

The apartment was a cozy two bedroom with a large living room and a grand kitchen. They visualized having parties and inviting lots of friends. As soon as they were settled, they called Sophie and acted surprised when she told them she was engaged. Sarah was extremely happy for her sister and asked when would the wedding day be? Sophie replied, Christmas Eve. Oh how wonderful Sarah said. After a few more questions from Sophie, about the honeymoon, they made plans to meet at Frankie's restaurant with her and Dave. Later at Frankie's over drinks and pizza, John congratulated Dave on the engagement. Dave and Sophie wanted to know everything about the honeymoon. John just laughed and said, a gentleman never tells. Sarah said they had so much fun, we went paragliding and whale watching. The next half hour, John couldn't stop talking about the dinner cruise. He told them about all the whales they had spotted in the ocean. Dave and Sophie hearing the excitement in John's voice, listened with delight. Sarah could barely get a word in edgewise, but did say she would do it again in a heart beat. John could only hear, his heartbeat is very week. The doctor was doing everything in his power to save John's life. Deep down, John knew it was futile to waste all that energy on him. John knew he wasn't going to make it, and that was okay.

Chapter 9

FATHERS ADVICE

John was twenty five when Samantha was born, and Sarah was so happy to have a girl. They had tried for two years to have a child, but no matter what they tried, it wasn't working. Sarah was dismayed and ready to give up, so she talked to John about adopting a child. John was very sad to see Sarah so unhappy so he decided to visit Father Thomas. John told Father about being unable to have a baby, and was shocked at the response Father gave him. John, have you asked Jesus for a child? Well no, John answered. Sarah and I were so busy trying to make it happen, we never asked for God's help. John, Father stated, you know all good things come from God, you also know what the bible say's. The verse that tells us, where two or three are gathered in my name, there I am in their midst. Jesus is here with us now John, ask and you shall receive. Let's pray John. John began this way, Jesus, I'm so sorry for not asking for your blessing by giving us a child. I'm sorry for not trusting you. Please Lord, have compassion on your servants, and grant Sarah and I a child to bring joy into our lives. Father Thomas said, Amen. John's faith exploded to the point where he just knew in his heart his request would be granted. When John got home, he told Sarah what had occurred with Father Thomas and Jesus. The biggest smile ever came on Sarah's face, as a faith filled surge came over her, and she believed. The very next month, at her doctors appointment, she was told the news, she was pregnant. She was on cloud nine, and couldn't wait to get home and tell John. After work, John came home and smelled his favorite dish wafting thru the air. Kissing Sarah and saying hello, he asked, what's the occasion for pot roast? She held John close, and whispered in his ear, I am especially hungry tonight, as I'm eating for two. John heard her words but they didn't register. He stepped back and looked at Sarah's huge smile, then the light came on. You mean, are we having a baby? No, Sarah answered, you and the Holy Spirit did your part, I'm having the baby. During dinner they talked about the dreams they both had for their baby. Would it be a boy or a girl and what effect on the world would their child have.

Samantha was born eight months later, and Sarah had no problems what so ever. The baby was a real trooper, and didn't fuss at all. John was so proud of Sarah as he watched Samantha lay on her moms belly, her tiny hands and feet wrapped in mittens and socks, sleeping so peacefully. Coming home from the hospital three days later, was the highlight for Sarah, as she had been cooped up for too long. Little Samantha was sleeping in the car seat when Sarah asked John to stop at the corner store. John asked Sarah what she needed, and she replied, oh I'll know it when I see it. What? John said, you aren't going in are you? Oh honey I feel fine, I'll only be a few minutes. You're serious, aren't you? John asked surprised. Sarah replied, I will be out before Samantha wakes up, don't worry so much daddy. That strong will is what John admired so much about Sarah. The welcome home party for Sarah and Samantha was wonderful, with all their friends and family gathered together. John had the party catered, so no one had to lift a finger, and just enjoy themselves. Everybody was surprised to see how much Samantha looked like her mom, and how beautiful she was. John was the proudest dad on earth, and thanked everyone for their dear comments. Samantha just slept thru it all. After the party had ended, and all the guests had left, John and Sarah sat on the couch talking about how blessed they were. Then they thanked Jesus for fulfilling their prayer.

The next two years were uneventful as Samantha grew like a weed. John and Sarah were treasuring every moment of those baby years. Samantha was learning new things every day, like walking by eighteen months. Then as Samantha was about to turn two years old, Sarah did something out of the ordinary, again. She served pot roast at the birthday party. Um, isn't that a strange dish to serve at a birthday party? John asked Sarah. Sarah looked at John and smiled while nodding her head. Really, John asked, another baby? Sarah said, you bet stud. John hugged Sarah and Samantha with joy boiling over. Joshua was the cutest little boy, he resembled John in many ways. His nose, his eyes, even his hair color and demeanor matched his dads. Joshua was a toy to Samantha, she would tickle him and watch him giggle for hours on end. Watching Samantha tickle Joshua, John felt a tickle on his foot, he tried to see who was doing that, but he couldn't move. The restraints on the bed held him tight, and John wondered why he was tied down. Then he heard the doctor say, why are you tickling his foot? A familiar voice said, that's how he will know it's me. Samantha, John mouthed, but couldn't get the word out. Sam came to the head of the bed and looked down at her dad. Tears were streaming down her cheeks, as she took her fathers hand in hers. Dad, if you can hear me squeeze my hand. John tried with all the strength he could muster, but couldn't squeeze his daughters hand. When Sam was a toddler, John would pick her up and say, I love you, then he would razzberry her belly. Sam would shoot back with a giggle, I love you more daddy, and razzberry his neck. Sam leaned in close to her fathers ear and said, I love you more daddy. Then moving down to Her Dad's neck she razzberried his neck. John squeezed Sam's hand and fell back into his dreams.

Chapter 10

LOST

John's dream took him back to the camping trip they had all taken to the Catskills. Joshua was only eight then, but full of curiosity. John remembered setting up the tent with Sarah, as Samantha was emptying out the car. Joshua had wandered off, chasing after a squirrel he had seen gathering nuts. Joshua had followed that critter into the woods for quite awhile, when he realized he was lost. After wandering around looking for the way back to the campsite, he became very frightened, and started to cry out. He started running thinking he would find the right direction to go. But he didn't. He became not only hopelessly lost, but now he was exhausted.

John and Sarah, after setting up the tent, looked around for Joshua, but when he didn't respond to their calls, they became quite concerned. They asked Samantha if she had seen her brother, but she said no. Joshua was no where in sight. Joshua stopped running and began to calm down. He sat down on the forest floor and tried to remember what his dad had taught him on those trips into the deep woods. John would periodically take Joshua with him as he worked. Scouting trails and looking for injured animals was part of John's job, and Joshua was safe tagging along with him. When John's job was more dangerous, like looking for poachers, he would leave Joshua at home. Joshua had learned many survival skills on those trips, and he would need them now. As Joshua thought back, he remembered his dad saying, never run when you are lost. Keep your cool and try to relax. Look to the Sun for directions. Look which side of a tree the moss is growing. Always walk down stream if you find water. Suddenly, Joshua felt at ease. Travel on game trails in thick forests, his dad would say. Look for campsites with wood and water, if possible. Water is your number one priority. Joshua listened intently for the sound of moving water. Not hearing any, he got up and started walking in a straight direction. He had picked out a mountain peak he saw in the distance, and kept it right in front of him as he walked. After about a quarter of an hour, Joshua heard the faint trickle of water. One hundred yards further, he found the stream he heard. Joshua knew his family was camping along side a lake surrounded by mountains. He figured this stream would eventually make it's way into that lake. As dusk was approaching, Joshua decided to make camp for the night, then in the morning he would follow that stream to the lake.

He looked around and spotted a huge pine tree with low hanging branches. Using his pocket knife, he cut off some of the lower branches. Then he crisscrossed them into the slightly higher limbs, to make a kind of roof. Then finding a nearby pine, he cut off more branches to make a floor. For an eight year old boy, Joshua was not only brave, but surprisingly skilled in the woods. Thanks to his dads teaching. After making his shelter, Joshua remembered what his dad had told him about survival, shelter, fire, water. He had made his shelter, and the stream provided all the water he needed, now he lacked one thing. His dad had shown Joshua how to make fire with a bow drill, unfortunately, he didn't have one. Joshua looked around for the right ingredients to make a bow drill. He found some hard wood and a flat rock for the base. He needed rope to complete the instrument. He had no rope and became discouraged and lowered his head to the ground. Unexpectedly, he found just what he needed. Shoe laces on his boots would work just fine. Joshua gathered small dry twigs for kindling. Then he went down to the stream in search of a certain plant his dad told him about. He hit pay dirt as he gazed on pussy willows, lining the stream. He grabbed a few and made his way back to his camp site. Breaking down the plants into a fine fabric, he knew he had the fuel he needed. Next, using a small rock, Joshua chipped away a pocket into the flat stone. This would hold the fabric and the bottom of his upright stick. He bent a pine bow, and using his shoelace, made a small curved bow. Next he wrapped the shoelace around the upright stick. Holding the stick in place, he used a smaller flat rock on top. Then with one hand holding the top rock down, he used his other hand to move the bow back and forth, spinning the stick. It seemed like hours of moving that bow back and forth, that Joshua noticed a wisp of smoke rising from the plant fabric. A few seconds later, and billows of smoke began to appear. He stopped the bow and leaned down, gently blowing on the tiny ember until it burst into a wonderous flame. He remembered what his dad had said, go slow. Joshua slowly and gently took the tiny ember and placed it on the bundle of kindling. As the flame grew bigger, Joshua added larger sticks to the fire. He knew his dad would be proud of him.

John, Sarah, and Samantha, after searching for Joshua for over an hour became fearful, when they had no luck locating him. John called George Markam and asked for help. John became hopeful when George and a team of rangers arrived at the lake shortly there after. Before the rangers spread out to form a search party, Sarah led them all in a prayer. Jesus, please keep Joshua safe, and guide these compassionate men to his location. Amen. Two hours later, one of the rangers smelled smoke.

After discerning the direction of the smoke, he came upon a fire that was smoldering. Next to that fire, under a pine tree shelter, he found a little boy fast asleep. Sarah and John were elated when the news came over the walkie talkie that Joshua was found. Following the rangers directions, they soon were reunited with their son. When they arrived, Joshua ran to them for hugs and kisses. He told his mom and dad all about his adventure, following the squirrel, and getting lost. John was proud of the skills Joshua had used to stay alive. He marveled at the shelter Joshua had built, and how he had started a fire with no matches. As they all walked back to reunite with Samantha, Sarah thanked God for bringing back Joshua safe and sound. At the rescue staging area, a dozen rangers were standing along side George Markam. Sarah and John thanked them all for finding their son, and invited them all to their home the next day for a picnic celebration. They all agreed to attend if Joshua promised to stop chasing squirrels. Samantha was glued to her brother in a hug, which Sarah and John soon joined in on. That hug triggered something in John, the feeling he couldn't breath. He started coughing and gasping for breath, as reality had set in once again. He was in that white room coughing into an oxygen mask covering his face. John heard someone say, his oxygen levels are dropping. He passed out again and returned to his dream world.

Chapter 11

MR. JENKINS

When Samantha turned sixteen, John began teaching her how to drive, on Sara's blue Camry. John would bring Samantha to a desolate parking lot at a near by shopping mall. Being Sunday, it was hardly used, and was a safe place to teach her the basics. John was a little nervous as Samantha went a bit crookety forward, and a lot slithery backwards. After about a half hour she was starting to get the hang of it. John decided it was time for her to make some turns, which Samantha quickly mastered. After an hours lesson, John asked her if she was as hungry for lunch as he was. With a hard brake, and a giggle, she said you bet. During lunch at Taco Bell, Samantha discussed her plans for college with her dad. She knew from an early age she wanted to study aquatic life, and become a marine biologist. John had always loved the sea and was delighted when Samantha said she would be following in his dream job. They talked about Joshua and his plans on becoming an archaeologist. Joshua was always asking to go to the local museum, and would devour any knowledge about dinosaurs he could. He would spend hours picking the minds of the curator and his staff. They all knew Joshua on a first name basis and liked him a lot.

Sarah would encourage both children to pursue their dreams, and would never stifle their passion for learning. Samantha and Joshua were becoming young adults any parent would be proud of. After the driving lesson and lunch John drove them home. When he turned onto their street, he noticed his neighbor, Paul Jenkin's, mowing his lawn. John pulled over and Paul turned off the mower, and came to the curb to visit. Hey John, who is the young woman you have with you today? Samantha blushed and smiled at Mr. Jenkin's. This was my chauffeur for the day Paul. She took me driving around the Mall, so she could show me all the stores she spends my money at. They laughed at that and Paul said, I thought spending your money was Sarah's job. It's becoming a joint effort John replied. After inquiring about Annie, Paul's wife who was in a battle with cancer, Paul answered we are taking it one day at a time. She has good days, and bad days. John said to Paul, you know Sarah and I are praying Annie gets well soon. Paul stiffened up and said, you know my feelings on that subject. If there were a God, he wouldn't have let her get cancer in the first place. Paul and Annie had a daughter Emily, who would be graduating high school soon and would be attending the community college in the Fall. Annie would barely make Emily's graduation when the cancer would get the best of her. Oh by the way, Paul asked, what's Joshua doing digging up your back yard? I had better go find out, as he started the car and pulled into his driveway. As John and Samantha rounded the back of the house, there was Joshua, shovel in hand, making a large hole in the yard. Joshua, John yelled, what are you doing? Digging for dino bones, he shot back. Fill in that hole this minute young man, John said. I will take you to a real dig site next weekend, how would that be? Woo hoo was all the fourteen year could say. That was one of John's favorite days to remember, his whole life. That was the day he made both his kids happy. Samantha and Joshua's dreams would become reality.

Reality he thought for a split second. Then it dawned on him, his reality was right here, right now, in this emergency room. As John came to once again, he felt a tremendous amount of pain. Two of his ribs were broken, and he had punctured a lung. That's why he couldn't breath very well. His shoulder was dislocated and his right leg was fractured. As he lay there restrained, he asked God to ease his pain. Just then a nurse who appeared to be glowing, started John on a morphine drip. Thank you Jesus for this angel, John said. Then fell back to sleep.

Chapter 12

FALLING AWAY

A few years later when the kids were both in college and Sarah's career was blooming, she was promoted to head nurse at the hospital. Something happened that would totally change the relationship Sarah and John had with Paul Jenkin's. You see, Sarah had been working the night shift, when she was called to come to room 103. There was a code red, and that meant something bad was happening. Sarah was aware Annie Jenkin's was in that room and knew what shape she was in. As Sarah walked thru the door the floor nurse told her Annie was near death. Sarah went to Annie's side and held her hand while talking to her. Annie, Sarah began, it will be alright. You need to know Jesus is waiting for you, and will take all your pain away. He loves you and wants you to be with him in Paradise. Will you accept Jesus as you Savior and receive His gift of life. With tears in her eyes, Annie said yes. Sarah hugged Annie and with that, she died in Sarah's arms.

Paul was devastated, and when John tried to tell him Annie was in a better place Paul snapped. He began yelling at John about how cruel his god was. How could any god kill his wife and expect praise. Don't ever talk to me again John. You can take your jesus with you. John was heart broken, and asked Jesus to forgive his neighbor. John never stopped praying for Paul.

Life seemed to roll along, and John and Sarah spent a lot of time with the kids. On weekends they would go on a picnic, or to a concert. During Spring break the four of them would spend vacations in different places around the country. In the Fall, the family would go picking blue berries and raspberries. Sarah enjoyed making jam, which went well with the pancakes on Sunday mornings. In the winter, John would take Joshua deer hunting, while the girls would spend their time shopping for the latest fashions. The family would attend Mass at St. Joseph's Catholic Church, every Sunday, but little by little Sarah and John began noticing a change in Joshua. While Sam would enjoy the Mass, participating in the songs and listening intently to the Gospel readings, Joshua became distant and aloof. Some Sundays he would feign sickness so as not to attend church.

Sarah and John became concerned regarding Joshua's behavior. Sarah asked Joshua straight out if he was losing faith in God. Both, John and Sarah were surprised at his response. I really don't believe in God or Jesus, he exclaimed. He went on to say, being a senior in college, we learn the truth. All the professors in my field of study agree, there couldn't possibly be a god, as the proof isn't there. Dinosaurs are real, he continued, bones are proof. Carbon dating gives us the age of the earth in billions of years. The absurdity of the bible claims the earth is six thousand years old. Come on, get real, where are Jesus's bones? You can't expect me to believe magic took him up into thin air, bones and all. Look, I am going to be an archaeologist, and I would be laughed out of my field if I believed fairy tales instead of facts. Sarah and John, in hind sight, had seen this coming but were still floored by Joshua's total non belief. Well, Joshua asked, what's the answer? OK, they both said to Joshua, we will not interfere with your beliefs, and if you don't want to attend church, it's your choice, you're an adult now. That day was the beginning of Sarah and John's transformation regarding their prayer life. Now, it was all hands on deck, including Sam, as they all prayed for Joshua's salvation. Years later, both parents would remain saddened by Joshua's choice, but they continued praying. Sam turned twenty four when she graduated college with a masters degree in marine biology. Because she was an honor student, she was quickly offered a position with Sealab, a New York based company. Sealab did research on marine animals exposed to chemical and oil spills. Sealab, had headquarters on Long Island, so Sam relocated there. It was only a three hour drive from her mom and dads house.

Joshua and three of his professors were at a dig site in Egypt for the summer. The grant the college was fortunate to acquire from the Federal Government, would supply all their equipment, food, lodging, and personnel expenses. Sarah would worry, whenever the children left home, and now her anxiety level went into the stratosphere, as she and John became empty nesters.

Chapter 13

TRAVELING

In time Sarah adjusted to her new life with John. They began traveling to distant locations, Sarah felt as if they were honeymooning over and over again. Camping became a thing of the past. Sarah and John went on a ten day Caribbean cruise, which both thought was more fun than the Bahamas. They could gamble all night long if they wanted. They could see shows, or play shuffleboard, see a movie, or relax on the deck with a drink But the best thing about the cruise, was the food. From fine dining in the great hall, to a hamburger and fries on deck after a swim. One night they had a seafood buffet which consisted of lobster, shrimp, scallops, clams, mussels and a variety of other fish. That meal was by far the highlight of the cruise. John told Sarah he had gained five pounds in that one night. It's the gym for you in the morning tubby.

The next year they traveled to France and Italy. John just fell in love with Venice, and the allure of the water. They took a gondola ride which Sarah thought was very romantic as the Italian man would sing to them. He told them every time they went under a bridge, it was customary for them to kiss. Sarah would fall in love all over again, with each bridge. One day they walked over the beautiful Rialto Bridge, and Sarah couldn't resist but kiss John. The gondolier did say under and over all bridges, didn't he? John was happy to agree. The churches were especially beautiful, the oldest, Chiesa di San Giacomo di Rialto, dates back to the year 421. John and Sarah both loved St. Marks Cathedral, which was completed in the 15th century. Their next stop was Pisa, where they visited the Pisa Cathedral, one of the most impressive churches in Tuscany. A masterpiece of Pisan Romanesque architecture, chiefly famous for its bell tower. The leaning tower of Pisa. John and Sarah were stunned to see people actually walking on top of that tower. Across from the tower sat the Pisa Baptistery, the interior is very simple and without decorations, but has exceptional acoustics. Galieo Galilei was baptized there in 1564. Sarah and John were amazed when an opera singer entered and sang one note. As they listened she soon sang another note. With the acoustics it sounded as if she were accompanied by another singer. Her voice reverberated all around the dome.

In Florence they saw the Statue of The David in pure white marble. That same museum had a painting of Abraham ready to slay his son Isaac, while an angel held back his arm holding the knife. A ram was caught in a thicket nearby. Both being Christians, they knew that ram was a representative of Jesus. Sarah and John both teared up while gazing at that portrait of Abraham's obedience to God. From there they boarded a train which the guide said the white on top of that mountain isn't snow. It is white marble, used to create The David and many other beautiful statues. As John and Sarah looked ahead they could see a huge mountain directly in front of the train. They wondered how they would get around it. That question was answered right away when they went through a tunnel under that mountain. What a grand experience they thought as they exited the far side and looked back to see the mountain disappearing in the distance. As their time in Italy was ending, they took a short bus ride to Nice, in the South of France. The small hills they passed, were lined round and round with grape vines and olive trees. It seemed every hill top had a Church or Castle. They arrived in nice which was nestled into a cove, with colorful houses wrapped around and above the town. Cliffs were dotted with those houses which looked down on the Mediterranean Ocean. After checking into their motel, they decided to walk along the beach. They noticed two different color blues in the water. They also heard a strange noise coming from the shore line. Walking down to the waters edge, they heard a rolling crackling sound. Creeda oop, then creeda aah. Round stones the size of grapefruits lined the beach in layers. When the tide came in, the stones rolled over one another making one noise. Then when the tide rolled out the stones it made a different noise. Oh the wonders of our God they thought.

John and Sarah would never forget these sights and sounds.

After two days in nice, John and Sarah would be departing for Paris. Arriving at the train station, they noticed the engine car was very streamlined, and they wondered why. They would soon find out, as the train picked up more and more speed. They would be going over two hundred miles per hour. The passenger cars were double deckers, and John and Sarah picked the upper deck to see the sights. They looked out the window as cars in the distance seemed to be traveling backwards, even though they were heading in the same direction. John went forward to get something from the dinning car for Sarah. As he walked near a window, he could see the country side going by, somewhat slowly. Then he looked down to see some cows standing near the tracks behind a fence. Whoa, the ground was speeding by at two hundred and twenty miles an hour. John became a little dizzy, and quickly looked away. Wow that's fast he thought.

Arriving in Paris, Sarah took one look around, and fell in love all over again. The next day would be spent shopping, not John's favorite thing to do, but he dutifully carried the bags for Sarah. Getting around the city was easy when they mastered the Paris metro train system, which traveled under ground, all around Paris. One minute they were at the Louvre, a few minutes later, they would pop up from the ground at the Eiffel Tower. John's absolute best experience, was at San Chappelle Cathedral. The church was constructed in 1248, and only took seven years to build. Sainte Chapelle was intended to house precious Christian relics, including Christ's crown of thorns, aquired by Saint Louis. John was amazed by the spiral staircase winding up to the main worship area, which was surrounded by stained glass windows depicting the story of the books of the Bible, from Genesis on the left hand side, right round to the book of Revelation on the Rose window to the rear. On the lower level, Mary's Chapel was breath taking, as you could feel her presence, and the love for her son radiated through out the room.

Sarah wished Joshua were here to feel God's presence. She knelt down and said a prayer for her son. Jesus please fill Joshua with your Spirit. Just then Sarah felt the whole church begin to shake. John do you feel that? She asked. Feel what he replied? The whole church is shaking she replied, do you feel it. No, John said, and just smiled at his wive who had never looked more beautiful.

John felt remorse they had to leave that place. He felt remorse for all the pain Jesus had to endure. Remorse was still on his mind as the morphine began to wear off. He especially felt remorse for Joshua's decision to live a life with out Jesus. His body was writhing in pain, but his mind was on his son. What was it Joshua had said to him in the ambulance, on their way to the hospital? As John went in and out of consciousness, he couldn't focus on Joshua's words. He tried to concentrate on the beginning of the days events leading up to this place. He couldn't, and fell back into the dream.

Chapter 14

FORGIVENESS

The years seemed to fly by, and both John and Sarah settled into a routine of visiting Samantha and Joshua on holidays and birthdays. Both children, now adults, had rewarding professions. Samantha a Marine Biologist, and Joshua an Archaeologist. John and Sarah were extremely proud of both of them. It was Samantha's fortieth birthday, and all the family had gathered to celebrate. Sam's husband, along with their son and daughter had come. Sam's mother and father in law had also came for the party. Joshua had never married, but his girl friend, Vanessa, had come. Everyone was enjoying them selves, when Sarah realized they were out of whipped cream, and asked John if he would go to the corner store, and get some. Sure honey, John said, Joshua, would you like to walk along with you're old dad, in case I fall down? Sure dad, we could race like we did when you were in shape, he chided. John said, your old man still has some moves, and gave Joshua a baby punch in his arm. Ouch, Joshua yelled, in fake pain. As they started walking, they spotted Mr. Jenkins out watering his lawn. He was across the street, and his grandson, Bobby, had crossed the street to their side, to retrieve his ball. Dad, Joshua said, did you ever stop pestering Mr. Jenkin's about Jesus? We haven't spoken in many years, since Mrs. Jenkin's died. He told me, he would never to speak to me again. I never stopped praying for him, or you son. My prayer for you every day, is that Jesus touches you in such a way that you would be certain he is real, and that he loves you.

Just then, a car came racing around the corner, at the same time Bobby was crossing the street, back to his grandpa. The car was out of control, and Bobby was directly in it's path. Quickly and with out thinking, John dashed into the street. Dad, no, is all Joshua could yell, but to no avail. Joshua watched as his father pushed Bobby out of the road. He was helpless as he saw his dad hit by the car. John was thrown into the air, as Joshua looked on horrified. When he came to his senses, he ran to his father and held him in his arms. John's broken and bleeding body was limp, and seemed lifeless. Joshua yelled to Mr. Jenkin's to call 911 and get help here fast. Father, Joshua whispered, Mr. Jenkin's hated you because of your faith ramblings, why did you save his grandson? John opened his eyes for just a moment, looked with compassion at his son, and said in a weak voice. Love you neighbor. Joshua started crying as something in him changed at that moment. Years later, Joshua found out Paul Jenkin's had found God, and became a Deacon. Deacon Paul would preach about Jesus at the same church Joshua attended as a child.

As Joshua was cradling his father in his arms, The Lord spoke to him. Just like my sons sacrifice, your fathers sacrifice saves. Honor your father and turn to me, and live. Joshua had received the sign John had prayed for in that church, years ago in Paris. Joshua wept. He turned back to the Lord and accepted Jesus as his Savior. A few years later, while visiting his mother on a Sunday, he asked if she would attend mass at St. Josephs with him. She said yes, and smiled at her son. Deacon Paul Jenkin's was giving the homily, while Sarah and Joshua listened intently. H started by saying, God was never real to him. He continued saying, when his wife Annie had died, he hated God, who was never there when he was needed. I blamed God for killing Sarah. When my neighbor John tried to convert me before Annie died, I felt disdain towards John. He just kept on preaching to me year after year. Then when she died John tried to console me, I yelled at John to stay out of my life and never talk to me ever again.

Deacon Jenkin's began to choke up, and with tears in his eyes continued. John threw himself in front of a speeding car to save my grandson, from certain death. Deacon Jenkin's broke down and started crying. John never gave up on me or my family. On that fateful day, I found Jesus, because of John's sacrifice. Sarah and Joshua were both in tears, as they came forward to hug Deacon Jenkin's.

Chapter 15

THE ANSWER

John woke up and was thinking about the day, and what Joshua had said to him in the ambulance. Then his mind cleared, and he remembered. Dad, I believe Jesus is Lord, I always have. Even in my rebellious years, please forgive me. John, remembered he had smiled and squeezed his son's hand. His prayers had been answered.

Sarah was at his side, when John came to for the last time. John, Sarah said, I love you with all my heart and soul. I will always love you and want you with me. But I can't be selfish and keep you from Jesus. It's time to say goodbye for a little while. Are you ready? John looked lovingly into Sarah's eyes, and passed away.

At John's funeral, his friends and family, gathered to say goodbye. Deacon Jenkin's placed a cross on the casket, which was made out of two willow sticks, Sarah had given him from Old Man Willow. Samantha and her husband and children, placed some sand on the casket. Joshua was sobbing when he came near his father. He fell to his knees and said, Thank you dad, for giving me THE ANSWER. Joshua had finally found the answer, the day his father sacrificed his life to save a little boy. If you confess with your lips Jesus is Lord, and believe in your heart, God raised him from the dead, you will be saved. Amen

Printed in the United States
by Baker & Taylor Publisher Services